What Are the Branches of Government?

by Jennifer Boothroyd

first step nonfiction

Lerner Publications ◆ Minneapolis

LERNER

SOURCE

Expand learning beyond the printed book. Download free, complementary educational resources for this book from our website, www.lernerresource.com.

The images in this book are used with the permission of: © Everett Collection Inc/Alamy, p. 4; © Yoon S. Byun/The Boston Globe/Getty Images, p. 5; © Blend Images/Hill Street Studios/Getty Images, p. 6; © iStockphoto.com/VisualField, pp. 7 (left), 9; © Image Source/Digital Vision/Thinkstock, pp. 7 (right), 20; AP Photo/Carolyn Kaster, p. 7 (middle); © Mark Wilson/Getty Images, p. 8; © Mark Wilson/Getty Images, p. 10; AP Photo/Jessica Hill, p. 11; © Olivier Douliery-Pool/Getty Images, p. 12; Ron Sachs/CNP/Newscom, p. 13; © Joshua Lott/AFP/Getty Images, p. 14; © Chip Somodevillay/Getty Images, p. 15; © Jeffery Isaac Greenberg/Alamy, p. 16; AP Photo/Kent D. Jonhson/Atlanta Journal-Constitution, p. 17; © Joe Burbank/Orlando Sentinel/Getty Images, p. 18; © Chip Somodevilla/Getty Images, p. 19; © Brendan Smialowski/Getty Images, p. 21; © Mandel Ngan/AFP/Getty Images, p. 22. Front cover: © iStockphoto.com/cristinaciochina.

Main body text set in ITC Avant Garde Gothic Std Medium 21/25.
Typeface provided by Adobe Systems.

Lerner Publications Company
A division of Lerner Publishing Group, Inc.
241 First Avenue North
Minneapolis, MN 55401 USA

For reading levels and more information, look up this title at www.lernerbooks.com.

Library of Congress Cataloging-in-Publication Data

Boothroyd, Jennifer, 1972–
    What are the branches of government? / by Jennifer Boothroyd.
        pages cm. — (First step nonfiction—exploring government)
    Includes index.
    ISBN 978-1-4677-8573-0 (lb : alk. paper) — ISBN 978-1-4677-8619-5 (pb : alk. paper) — ISBN 978-1-4677-8620-1 (eb pdf)
    1. United States—Politics and government—Juvenile literature. [1. United States—Politics and government.] I. Title.
JK40.H36 2016
320.473'04—dc23   2014041109

Manufactured in the United States of America
2-43813-19280-3/20/2017

Table of Contents

What Is Government?

Our country is run by a government.

This girl meets her state's senator.

The government works for us.

We vote for our leaders.

We choose the people in our government.

Government branches have different jobs.

Our government has three branches.

The branches work together.

Each branch has some power. But no branch has all the power.

Congress is in charge of one branch.

Leaders from each state make up Congress.

We must follow the laws Congress makes.

They work together to make laws.

11

The President and the Cabinet

The **president** leads another branch.

The president
limits the power
of Congress.

The president must **approve** new laws.

The FBI is part of the president's branch.

The president's branch makes sure that people follow laws.

14

The **cabinet** is a group that helps the president.

Taking care of parks is a service.

The cabinet is in charge of many **services**.

The third branch runs the **courts**.

This branch decides if someone broke a law.

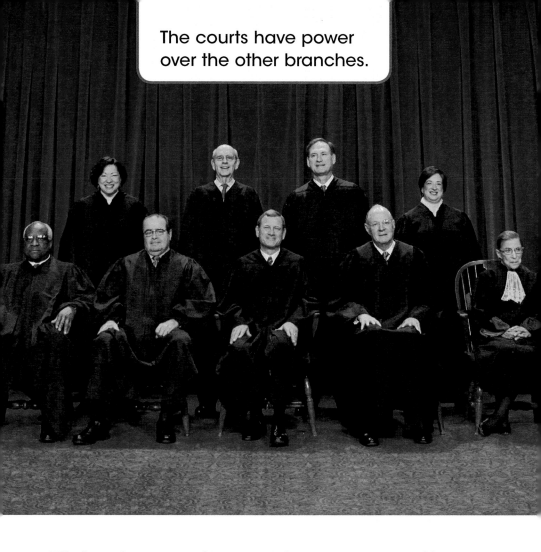

The courts have power over the other branches.

This branch makes sure the other branches follow laws.

Judges are in charge of the courts.

Congress must approve judges chosen by the president.

The president chooses some judges.

The government runs well
when the branches work
together.

Glossary

approve – to agree with or accept

cabinet – a group of people who help the president

Congress – people elected from each state who make the laws for the country

courts – places where legal cases are heard and decided

president – the leader of one branch of government

services – jobs people do to help others

Index